50 Ice Cream Flavors from Around the World

By: Kelly Johnson

Table of Contents

- Matcha (Japan)
- Black Sesame (Japan)
- Ube (Philippines)
- Durian (Southeast Asia)
- Taro (Taiwan)
- Red Bean (China)
- Mango Sticky Rice (Thailand)
- Hokey Pokey (New Zealand)
- Milo (Australia)
- Feijoa (New Zealand)
- Tim Tam (Australia)
- Kulfi (India)
- Rose (Middle East)
- Saffron and Pistachio (Iran)
- Turkish Coffee (Turkey)
- Halva (Middle East)
- Baklava (Turkey)
- Ricotta and Fig (Italy)
- Tiramisu (Italy)
- Stracciatella (Italy)
- Spaghettieis (Germany)
- Amarena Cherry (Italy)
- Speculoos (Belgium)
- Salted Licorice (Finland)
- Cloudberry (Scandinavia)
- Salmiakki (Finland)
- Lavender Honey (France)
- Chestnut (France)
- Brown Bread (Ireland)
- Guinness (Ireland)
- Clotted Cream (UK)
- Elderflower (UK)
- Maple Walnut (Canada)
- Tiger Tail (Canada)
- Beaver Tail (Canada)

- Cajeta (Mexico)
- Churro (Mexico)
- Corn (Mexico)
- Lucuma (Peru)
- Mate (Argentina)
- Dulce de Leche (Argentina)
- Cheese (Brazil)
- Tamarind (Colombia)
- Açaí (Brazil)
- Coconut (Caribbean)
- Rum Raisin (Jamaica)
- Black Forest (Germany)
- Melonpan (Japan)
- Pandan (Southeast Asia)
- Wasabi (Japan)

Matcha Ice Cream (Japan)

Ingredients:

- 2 cups heavy cream
- 1 cup whole milk
- ¾ cup sugar
- 2 tbsp matcha powder
- 4 egg yolks

Instructions:

1. Whisk egg yolks and sugar in a bowl until light and fluffy.
2. Heat milk and heavy cream in a saucepan over medium heat until warm (do not boil).
3. Slowly whisk the warm milk into the egg mixture, then return to the saucepan.
4. Stir in matcha powder and cook over low heat until slightly thickened.
5. Strain and chill in the refrigerator for 4 hours.
6. Churn in an ice cream maker according to manufacturer instructions.
7. Freeze for at least 2 hours before serving.

Black Sesame Ice Cream (Japan)

Ingredients:

- 1 cup whole milk
- 2 cups heavy cream
- ¾ cup sugar
- 4 egg yolks
- 3 tbsp black sesame paste

Instructions:

1. Whisk egg yolks and sugar until pale.
2. Heat milk and cream until warm, then slowly mix into the egg mixture.
3. Return to heat and cook until thickened.
4. Stir in black sesame paste until smooth.
5. Strain, chill for 4 hours, then churn in an ice cream maker.
6. Freeze for at least 2 hours before serving.

Ube Ice Cream (Philippines)

Ingredients:

- 2 cups heavy cream
- 1 cup whole milk
- ¾ cup sugar
- 1 cup ube halaya (purple yam jam)
- 1 tsp ube extract

Instructions:

1. Heat milk, sugar, and ube halaya in a saucepan until sugar dissolves.
2. Blend mixture until smooth, then stir in heavy cream and ube extract.
3. Chill for 4 hours, then churn in an ice cream maker.
4. Freeze for at least 2 hours before serving.

Durian Ice Cream (Southeast Asia)

Ingredients:

- 2 cups durian flesh, mashed
- 1 cup whole milk
- 1 cup heavy cream
- ½ cup sugar
- 2 egg yolks

Instructions:

1. Heat milk and sugar until sugar dissolves.
2. Blend with durian flesh until smooth.
3. Whisk egg yolks, then slowly mix in the warm milk.
4. Cook over low heat until thickened.
5. Stir in heavy cream, chill for 4 hours, then churn.
6. Freeze for at least 2 hours before serving.

Taro Ice Cream (Taiwan)

Ingredients:

- 1 cup taro root (peeled, diced)
- 2 cups heavy cream
- 1 cup whole milk
- ¾ cup sugar
- ½ tsp vanilla extract

Instructions:

1. Boil taro until soft, then mash into a smooth paste.
2. Heat milk and sugar until sugar dissolves.
3. Stir in mashed taro and blend until smooth.
4. Stir in heavy cream and vanilla, then chill for 4 hours.
5. Churn in an ice cream maker and freeze.

Red Bean Ice Cream (China)

Ingredients:

- 1 cup sweet red bean paste
- 2 cups heavy cream
- 1 cup whole milk
- ¾ cup sugar
- ½ tsp vanilla extract

Instructions:

1. Heat milk and sugar until sugar dissolves.
2. Stir in red bean paste and blend until smooth.
3. Stir in heavy cream and vanilla, then chill.
4. Churn in an ice cream maker, then freeze.

Mango Sticky Rice Ice Cream (Thailand)

Ingredients:

- 1 cup cooked sticky rice
- 1 cup mango purée
- 1 can coconut milk (13.5 oz)
- 1 cup heavy cream
- ¾ cup sugar

Instructions:

1. Heat coconut milk and sugar until sugar dissolves.
2. Stir in mango purée and mix well.
3. Stir in heavy cream, then chill for 4 hours.
4. Churn in an ice cream maker, adding sticky rice near the end.
5. Freeze before serving.

Hokey Pokey Ice Cream (New Zealand)

Ingredients:

- 2 cups heavy cream
- 1 cup whole milk
- ¾ cup sugar
- 1 tsp vanilla extract
- ½ cup honeycomb toffee (crushed)

Instructions:

1. Heat milk and sugar until sugar dissolves.
2. Stir in vanilla and heavy cream, then chill.
3. Churn in an ice cream maker, adding honeycomb near the end.
4. Freeze before serving.

Milo Ice Cream (Australia)

Ingredients:

- ½ cup Milo powder
- 2 cups heavy cream
- 1 cup whole milk
- ¾ cup sugar

Instructions:

1. Heat milk, sugar, and Milo powder until sugar dissolves.
2. Stir in heavy cream, then chill for 4 hours.
3. Churn in an ice cream maker, then freeze.

Feijoa Ice Cream (New Zealand)

Ingredients:

- 1 cup feijoa purée (scooped and blended)
- 2 cups heavy cream
- 1 cup whole milk
- ¾ cup sugar

Instructions:

1. Heat milk and sugar until sugar dissolves.
2. Stir in feijoa purée and mix well.
3. Stir in heavy cream, then chill.
4. Churn in an ice cream maker and freeze.

Tim Tam Ice Cream (Australia)

Ingredients:

- 2 cups heavy cream
- 1 cup whole milk
- ¾ cup sugar
- ½ cup cocoa powder
- ½ cup chopped Tim Tam biscuits

Instructions:

1. Heat milk, sugar, and cocoa powder until sugar dissolves.
2. Stir in heavy cream, then chill for 4 hours.
3. Churn in an ice cream maker, adding chopped Tim Tams near the end.
4. Freeze before serving.

Kulfi (India)

Ingredients:

- 4 cups whole milk
- ½ cup condensed milk
- ½ cup heavy cream
- ½ cup sugar
- ¼ tsp cardamom powder
- ¼ cup chopped pistachios
- ¼ tsp saffron strands (optional)

Instructions:

1. Heat milk in a saucepan over medium heat, stirring continuously, until it reduces by half.
2. Stir in condensed milk, heavy cream, sugar, cardamom, saffron, and pistachios.
3. Cook for another 10 minutes until thickened.
4. Pour into molds and freeze for at least 6 hours before serving.

Rose Ice Cream (Middle East)

Ingredients:

- 2 cups heavy cream
- 1 cup whole milk
- ¾ cup sugar
- 1 tsp rose water
- ¼ cup chopped pistachios (optional)
- A few drops of pink food coloring (optional)

Instructions:

1. Heat milk, sugar, and cream in a saucepan until sugar dissolves.
2. Remove from heat and stir in rose water and food coloring.
3. Chill for 4 hours, then churn in an ice cream maker.
4. Mix in pistachios, then freeze for at least 2 hours before serving.

Saffron and Pistachio Ice Cream (Iran)

Ingredients:

- 2 cups heavy cream
- 1 cup whole milk
- ¾ cup sugar
- ½ tsp saffron threads, soaked in 2 tbsp warm milk
- ¼ cup chopped pistachios
- ½ tsp vanilla extract

Instructions:

1. Heat milk, sugar, and saffron mixture until sugar dissolves.
2. Stir in heavy cream and vanilla extract.
3. Chill for 4 hours, then churn in an ice cream maker.
4. Mix in pistachios, then freeze for 2 hours before serving.

Turkish Coffee Ice Cream (Turkey)

Ingredients:

- 2 cups heavy cream
- 1 cup whole milk
- ¾ cup sugar
- 3 tbsp Turkish coffee (very finely ground)
- 4 egg yolks

Instructions:

1. Heat milk and sugar until sugar dissolves.
2. Stir in Turkish coffee and let steep for 10 minutes.
3. Strain and whisk into egg yolks.
4. Cook over low heat until thickened, then stir in heavy cream.
5. Chill for 4 hours, churn, and freeze for at least 2 hours.

Halva Ice Cream (Middle Eastern Inspired)

Ingredients:

- 2 cups heavy cream
- 1 cup whole milk
- ¾ cup sugar
- ½ cup crumbled halva (plain or pistachio)
- ½ tsp vanilla extract
- ¼ tsp sea salt
- ¼ cup tahini (optional, for extra sesame flavor)
- Chopped pistachios or sesame seeds for garnish

Instructions:

1. **Heat the base:** In a saucepan, heat the milk and sugar over medium heat until the sugar dissolves.
2. **Blend the flavors:** Stir in the tahini (if using) and crumbled halva, mixing until well combined.
3. **Add cream:** Remove from heat and stir in the heavy cream, vanilla, and sea salt.
4. **Chill:** Let the mixture cool completely in the refrigerator for at least 4 hours (or overnight for best results).
5. **Churn:** Pour the chilled mixture into an ice cream maker and churn according to the manufacturer's instructions.
6. **Fold in more halva:** In the last few minutes of churning, fold in additional crumbled halva for texture.
7. **Freeze:** Transfer to a container, sprinkle with chopped pistachios or sesame seeds, and freeze for at least 4 hours before serving.

Baklava Ice Cream (Turkey)

Ingredients:

- 2 cups heavy cream
- 1 cup whole milk
- ¾ cup sugar
- ½ tsp cinnamon
- ¼ cup chopped walnuts
- ¼ cup crushed phyllo pastry
- ¼ cup honey

Instructions:

1. Heat milk, sugar, and cinnamon until sugar dissolves.
2. Stir in heavy cream and chill for 4 hours.
3. Churn in an ice cream maker, then mix in walnuts and phyllo.
4. Drizzle honey on top before serving.

Ricotta and Fig Gelato (Italy)

Ingredients:

- 2 cups whole milk
- 1 cup heavy cream
- ¾ cup sugar
- 1 cup ricotta cheese
- 1 tsp vanilla extract
- ½ cup dried figs, chopped
- 2 tbsp honey
- 1 tbsp lemon zest

Instructions:

1. Heat the milk, heavy cream, and sugar in a saucepan until the sugar dissolves.
2. Blend in ricotta, vanilla, honey, and lemon zest until smooth.
3. Chill the mixture for at least 4 hours.
4. Churn in an ice cream maker according to instructions.
5. Fold in the chopped figs at the end.
6. Freeze for 4 hours before serving.

Tiramisu Gelato (Italy)

Ingredients:

- 2 cups whole milk
- 1 cup heavy cream
- ¾ cup sugar
- 3 egg yolks
- ½ cup mascarpone cheese
- ½ cup strong espresso
- 1 tbsp coffee liqueur (optional)
- 1 tsp vanilla extract
- Cocoa powder for dusting

Instructions:

1. Heat milk and sugar until warm, then whisk in egg yolks and cook until thickened.
2. Stir in espresso, coffee liqueur, and vanilla.
3. Blend in mascarpone until smooth.
4. Chill for 4 hours, churn, then freeze for 4 more hours.
5. Dust with cocoa powder before serving.

Stracciatella Gelato (Italy)

Ingredients:

- 2 cups whole milk
- 1 cup heavy cream
- ¾ cup sugar
- 1 tsp vanilla extract
- 4 oz dark chocolate, melted

Instructions:

1. Heat milk, cream, and sugar until dissolved, then add vanilla.
2. Chill the mixture, then churn in an ice cream maker.
3. Drizzle melted chocolate into the churning gelato to form thin streaks.
4. Freeze for 4 hours before serving.

Spaghettieis (Germany)

Ingredients:

- 2 cups vanilla ice cream
- ½ cup strawberry sauce
- 2 tbsp grated white chocolate
- Whipped cream (optional)

Instructions:

1. Place a layer of whipped cream on a plate.
2. Press softened vanilla ice cream through a potato ricer to resemble spaghetti.
3. Top with strawberry sauce and grated white chocolate.

Amarena Cherry Gelato (Italy)

Ingredients:

- 2 cups whole milk
- 1 cup heavy cream
- ¾ cup sugar
- 1 tsp vanilla extract
- ½ cup Amarena cherries, chopped
- ¼ cup Amarena cherry syrup

Instructions:

1. Heat milk, cream, and sugar until sugar dissolves.
2. Add vanilla, then chill the mixture.
3. Churn in an ice cream maker, then swirl in cherries and syrup.
4. Freeze for 4 hours before serving.

Speculoos Ice Cream (Belgium)

Ingredients:

- 2 cups heavy cream
- 1 cup whole milk
- ¾ cup sugar
- ½ cup Speculoos cookie butter
- 1 tsp cinnamon
- ½ cup crushed Speculoos cookies

Instructions:

1. Heat milk, cream, and sugar until warm.
2. Stir in cookie butter and cinnamon until smooth.
3. Chill, then churn in an ice cream maker.
4. Fold in crushed cookies before freezing.

Salted Licorice Ice Cream (Finland)

Ingredients:

- 2 cups heavy cream
- 1 cup whole milk
- ¾ cup sugar
- 2 tbsp black licorice syrup (or crushed salted licorice)
- ½ tsp sea salt
- 4 egg yolks

Instructions:

1. Heat milk, sugar, and licorice syrup in a saucepan until sugar dissolves.
2. Whisk egg yolks in a separate bowl, then slowly add the warm milk mixture while stirring.
3. Return to heat and cook until thickened.
4. Stir in heavy cream and salt, then chill for 4 hours.
5. Churn in an ice cream maker, then freeze for at least 2 hours before serving.

Cloudberry Ice Cream (Scandinavia)

Ingredients:

- 1 cup cloudberry jam or purée
- 2 cups heavy cream
- 1 cup whole milk
- ¾ cup sugar
- ½ tsp vanilla extract

Instructions:

1. Heat milk and sugar in a saucepan until sugar dissolves.
2. Stir in heavy cream and vanilla, then chill for 4 hours.
3. Churn in an ice cream maker, gradually adding the cloudberry jam.
4. Freeze for 2 hours before serving.

Salmiakki Ice Cream (Finland)

Ingredients:

- 2 cups heavy cream
- 1 cup whole milk
- ¾ cup sugar
- 2 tbsp crushed salmiakki candies
- 4 egg yolks

Instructions:

1. Heat milk, sugar, and crushed salmiakki in a saucepan until sugar dissolves.
2. Whisk egg yolks in a separate bowl and slowly add the warm milk mixture while stirring.
3. Return to heat and cook until thickened.
4. Stir in heavy cream and chill for 4 hours.
5. Churn in an ice cream maker, then freeze for 2 hours.

Lavender Honey Ice Cream (France)

Ingredients:

- 2 cups heavy cream
- 1 cup whole milk
- ¾ cup honey
- 2 tbsp dried lavender
- 4 egg yolks

Instructions:

1. Heat milk, honey, and lavender until warm. Remove from heat and let steep for 15 minutes.
2. Strain and whisk into egg yolks.
3. Cook over low heat until thickened.
4. Stir in heavy cream, chill for 4 hours, churn, then freeze for 2 hours.

Chestnut Ice Cream (France)

Ingredients:

- 1 cup chestnut purée
- 2 cups heavy cream
- 1 cup whole milk
- ¾ cup sugar
- ½ tsp vanilla extract

Instructions:

1. Heat milk and sugar until sugar dissolves.
2. Stir in chestnut purée and vanilla.
3. Chill for 4 hours, churn, and freeze for 2 hours.

Brown Bread Ice Cream (Ireland)

Ingredients:

- 2 cups heavy cream
- 1 cup whole milk
- ¾ cup sugar
- 1 cup toasted breadcrumbs
- ½ tsp cinnamon
- 4 egg yolks

Instructions:

1. Heat milk and sugar until sugar dissolves.
2. Whisk egg yolks separately, then slowly add warm milk.
3. Return to heat and cook until thickened.
4. Stir in heavy cream and chill for 4 hours.
5. Churn in an ice cream maker, adding toasted breadcrumbs near the end.
6. Freeze for 2 hours before serving.

Guinness Ice Cream (Ireland)

Ingredients:

- 1 cup Guinness stout
- 2 cups heavy cream
- 1 cup whole milk
- ¾ cup sugar
- 4 egg yolks

Instructions:

1. Simmer Guinness until reduced by half.
2. Heat milk and sugar until sugar dissolves.
3. Whisk egg yolks separately, then slowly add warm milk.
4. Return to heat and cook until thickened.
5. Stir in Guinness reduction and heavy cream, chill, churn, and freeze.

Clotted Cream Ice Cream (UK)

Ingredients:

- 1 cup clotted cream
- 2 cups heavy cream
- ¾ cup sugar
- 1 cup whole milk
- ½ tsp vanilla extract

Instructions:

1. Heat milk and sugar until sugar dissolves.
2. Stir in clotted cream and vanilla, chill for 4 hours, churn, and freeze.

Elderflower Ice Cream (UK)

Ingredients:

- ½ cup elderflower cordial
- 2 cups heavy cream
- 1 cup whole milk
- ¾ cup sugar

Instructions:

1. Heat milk and sugar until sugar dissolves.
2. Stir in elderflower cordial and cream.
3. Chill for 4 hours, churn, and freeze.

Maple Walnut Ice Cream (Canada)

Ingredients:

- 1 cup maple syrup
- 2 cups heavy cream
- 1 cup whole milk
- ¾ cup sugar
- ½ cup toasted walnuts

Instructions:

1. Heat milk and sugar until sugar dissolves.
2. Stir in maple syrup and heavy cream.
3. Chill for 4 hours, churn, and add walnuts.
4. Freeze for 2 hours before serving.

Tiger Tail Ice Cream (Canada)

Ingredients:

- 2 cups heavy cream
- 1 cup whole milk
- ¾ cup sugar
- 2 egg yolks
- 1 tsp vanilla extract
- 1 tsp orange zest
- ½ tsp orange extract
- Orange food coloring (optional)
- 2 tbsp black licorice syrup or finely chopped black licorice

Instructions:

1. Heat milk, sugar, and orange zest in a saucepan until sugar dissolves.
2. Whisk egg yolks separately, then slowly add warm milk mixture while stirring.
3. Return to heat and cook until thickened.
4. Stir in heavy cream, vanilla, and orange extract, then chill for 4 hours.
5. Churn in an ice cream maker, adding black licorice syrup in swirls near the end.
6. Freeze for 2 hours before serving.

Beaver Tail Ice Cream (Canada)

Ingredients:

- 2 cups heavy cream
- 1 cup whole milk
- ¾ cup sugar
- 1 tsp cinnamon
- ½ tsp nutmeg
- 4 egg yolks
- ½ cup crushed fried pastry pieces (or cinnamon-sugar-coated pie crust)

Instructions:

1. Heat milk, sugar, cinnamon, and nutmeg until sugar dissolves.
2. Whisk egg yolks separately, then slowly add warm milk mixture.
3. Return to heat and cook until thickened.
4. Stir in heavy cream, chill for 4 hours, then churn.
5. Add pastry pieces near the end and freeze for 2 hours before serving.

Cajeta Ice Cream (Mexico)

Ingredients:

- 1 cup cajeta
- 2 cups heavy cream
- 1 cup whole milk
- ¾ cup sugar
- ½ tsp vanilla extract

Instructions:

1. Heat milk, sugar, and cajeta until well blended.
2. Stir in vanilla and heavy cream.
3. Chill for 4 hours, churn, and freeze for 2 hours before serving.

Churro Ice Cream (Mexico)

Ingredients:

- 2 cups heavy cream
- 1 cup whole milk
- ¾ cup sugar
- 1 tsp cinnamon
- ½ tsp vanilla extract
- ½ cup chopped churros

Instructions:

1. Heat milk, sugar, and cinnamon until sugar dissolves.
2. Stir in vanilla and heavy cream, then chill.
3. Churn in an ice cream maker, adding chopped churros near the end.
4. Freeze for 2 hours before serving.

Corn Ice Cream (Mexico)

Ingredients:

- 2 ears fresh corn, kernels removed
- 2 cups heavy cream
- 1 cup whole milk
- ¾ cup sugar
- 4 egg yolks

Instructions:

1. Blend corn with milk until smooth, then strain.
2. Heat milk mixture with sugar until sugar dissolves.
3. Whisk egg yolks separately and add warm milk mixture while stirring.
4. Return to heat and cook until thickened.
5. Stir in heavy cream, chill for 4 hours, then churn and freeze.

Lucuma Ice Cream (Peru)

Ingredients:

- 1 cup lucuma purée
- 2 cups heavy cream
- 1 cup whole milk
- ¾ cup sugar
- ½ tsp vanilla extract

Instructions:

1. Heat milk and sugar until sugar dissolves.
2. Stir in lucuma purée and vanilla.
3. Chill for 4 hours, churn, and freeze.

Mate Ice Cream (Argentina)

Ingredients:

- 2 tbsp loose-leaf yerba mate
- 2 cups heavy cream
- 1 cup whole milk
- ¾ cup sugar
- 4 egg yolks

Instructions:

1. Steep yerba mate in warm milk for 15 minutes, then strain.
2. Heat milk with sugar until sugar dissolves.
3. Whisk egg yolks separately, then slowly add warm milk mixture.
4. Return to heat and cook until thickened.
5. Stir in heavy cream, chill for 4 hours, then churn and freeze.

Dulce de Leche Ice Cream (Argentina)

Ingredients:

- 1 cup dulce de leche
- 2 cups heavy cream
- 1 cup whole milk
- ¾ cup sugar
- ½ tsp vanilla extract

Instructions:

1. Heat milk, sugar, and dulce de leche until smooth.
2. Stir in vanilla and heavy cream, then chill.
3. Churn in an ice cream maker, then freeze for 2 hours.

Cheese Ice Cream (Brazil)

Ingredients:

- 1 cup shredded Minas cheese (or cream cheese)
- 2 cups heavy cream
- 1 cup whole milk
- ¾ cup sugar
- 4 egg yolks

Instructions:

1. Heat milk, sugar, and cheese until cheese melts.
2. Whisk egg yolks separately, then slowly add warm milk mixture.
3. Return to heat and cook until thickened.
4. Stir in heavy cream, chill for 4 hours, then churn and freeze.

Tamarind Ice Cream (Colombia)

Ingredients:

- 1 cup tamarind pulp (seedless)
- 2 cups heavy cream
- 1 cup whole milk
- ¾ cup sugar
- ½ tsp vanilla extract

Instructions:

1. Heat milk and sugar until sugar dissolves.
2. Stir in tamarind pulp and mix well.
3. Blend if necessary to ensure smooth consistency.
4. Stir in heavy cream and vanilla, then chill.
5. Churn in an ice cream maker, then freeze for 2 hours.

Açaí Ice Cream (Brazil)

Ingredients:

- 1 cup açaí purée
- 2 cups heavy cream
- 1 cup whole milk
- ¾ cup sugar
- 1 tbsp honey

Instructions:

1. Heat milk and sugar until sugar dissolves.
2. Stir in açaí purée and honey.
3. Blend until smooth.
4. Stir in heavy cream, then chill for 4 hours.
5. Churn in an ice cream maker, then freeze.

Coconut Ice Cream (Caribbean)

Ingredients:

- 1 can coconut milk (13.5 oz)
- 1 cup heavy cream
- ¾ cup sugar
- ½ tsp vanilla extract
- ½ cup shredded coconut (optional)

Instructions:

1. Heat coconut milk and sugar until sugar dissolves.
2. Stir in vanilla and heavy cream.
3. Chill for 4 hours, then churn.
4. Add shredded coconut near the end of churning.
5. Freeze for 2 hours before serving.

Rum Raisin Ice Cream (Jamaica)

Ingredients:

- ½ cup dark rum
- ½ cup raisins
- 2 cups heavy cream
- 1 cup whole milk
- ¾ cup sugar
- 4 egg yolks

Instructions:

1. Soak raisins in rum overnight.
2. Heat milk and sugar until sugar dissolves.
3. Whisk egg yolks separately, then add warm milk mixture while stirring.
4. Return to heat and cook until thickened.
5. Stir in heavy cream, chill for 4 hours, then churn.
6. Add rum-soaked raisins near the end and freeze.

Black Forest Ice Cream (Germany)

Ingredients:

- 2 cups heavy cream
- 1 cup whole milk
- ¾ cup sugar
- ½ cup cocoa powder
- ½ cup chopped cherries
- ¼ cup cherry liqueur (optional)
- ½ cup chocolate shavings

Instructions:

1. Heat milk, sugar, and cocoa powder until sugar dissolves.
2. Stir in heavy cream and cherry liqueur, then chill.
3. Churn in an ice cream maker, adding cherries and chocolate shavings near the end.
4. Freeze for 2 hours before serving.

Melonpan Ice Cream (Japan)

Ingredients:

- 2 cups heavy cream
- 1 cup whole milk
- ¾ cup sugar
- ½ tsp melon extract
- ½ cup crumbled melonpan (Japanese sweet bread)

Instructions:

1. Heat milk and sugar until sugar dissolves.
2. Stir in melon extract and heavy cream.
3. Chill for 4 hours, then churn.
4. Add crumbled melonpan near the end and freeze.

Pandan Ice Cream (Southeast Asia)

Ingredients:

- 1 cup pandan juice (blend pandan leaves with water and strain)
- 2 cups heavy cream
- 1 cup whole milk
- ¾ cup sugar
- ½ tsp vanilla extract

Instructions:

1. Heat milk, sugar, and pandan juice until sugar dissolves.
2. Stir in vanilla and heavy cream.
3. Chill for 4 hours, churn, and freeze.

Wasabi Ice Cream (Japan)

Ingredients:

- 2 cups heavy cream
- 1 cup whole milk
- ¾ cup sugar
- 1 tbsp wasabi paste

Instructions:

1. Heat milk and sugar until sugar dissolves.
2. Stir in wasabi paste, blending well.
3. Stir in heavy cream, then chill.
4. Churn in an ice cream maker, then freeze.

www.ingramcontent.com/pod-product-compliance
Lightning Source LLC
LaVergne TN
LVHW081339060526
838201LV00055B/2745